D0722310

Taipan/Taipán

By Shanya Worthy   Traducción al español: Nathalie Beullens

Gareth Stevens
Publishing

Please visit our Web site, www.garethstevens.com. For a free color catalog of all our high-quality books, call toll free 1-800-542-2595 or fax 1-877-542-2596.

Cataloging Data

Worthy, Shanya.
Taipan / Taipán
    p. cm. — (Killer snakes / Serpientes asesinas)
Includes index.
ISBN 978-1-4339-4569-4 (library binding)
1. Oxyuranus—Juvenile literature. I. Title.
QL666.O64W58 2010
597.96'4—dc22

                                          2010030694

First Edition

Published in 2011 by
Gareth Stevens Publishing
111 East 14th Street, Suite 349
New York, NY 10003

Copyright © 2011 Gareth Stevens Publishing

Designer: Michael J. Flynn
Editor: Greg Roza
Spanish translation: Nathalie Beullens

Photo credits: Cover, pp. 1, (2–4, 6–8, 10, 12, 14, 16, 18, 20–24 snake skin texture), 5, 9, 17 Shutterstock.com; pp. 6–7, 19 Brooke Watnall/National Geographic/Getty Images; p. 11 DEA/C.DANI-I.JESKE/De Agostini Picture Library/Getty Images; p. 13 Nicole Duplaix/National Geographic/Getty Images; p. 15 Jason Edwards/National Geographic/Getty Images; p. 21 iStockphoto.com.

Printed in the United States of America

CPSIA compliance information: Batch #CW11GS: For further information contact Gareth Stevens, New York, New York at 1-800-542-2595.

Contents

Contenido

Boldface words appear in the glossary/
Las palabras en **negrita** aparecen en el glosario

Types of Taipans

Three kinds of taipans live in Australia and New Guinea. Inland taipans live in the deserts of central Australia. Coastal taipans live along the northern coast of Australia and the southern coast of New Guinea. The Central Ranges taipan was just discovered in 2006!

Diferentes tipos de taipán

Hay tres clases de taipanes en Australia y Nueva Guinea. Los taipanes del interior viven en los desiertos de Australia central. Los taipanes de la costa viven a lo largo de la costa norte de Australia y la costa sur de la Nueva Guinea. ¡El taipán de la cordillera central recién fue descubierto en 2006!

KEY/CLAVE

coastal taipan/
taipán de la costa

inland taipan/
taipán del interior

Central Ranges taipan/
taipán de la cordillera central

New Guinea/
Nueva Guinea

Australia/
Australia

Taipan Bodies

The coastal taipan is the longest. Most grow to about 6 to 8 feet (1.8 to 2.4 m). They can be black, gray, or brown. Inland taipans are smaller. Most grow to about 5 feet (1.5 m) long. They are mostly brown or black.

El cuerpo de un taipán

El taipán de la costa es el más largo. La mayoría crece unos 6 a 8 pies (1.8 a 2.4 m). Puede ser negro, gris o marrón. Los taipanes del interior son más pequeños. La mayoría crece hasta unos 5 pies (1.5 m) de largo. La mayor parte son de color marrón o negro.

**coastal taipan/
taipán de la costa**

7

The Inland Taipan

The inland taipan lives in the desert where there are very few plants. It hides in cracks and under rocks. The taipan's **scales** are often darker in winter than in summer. This allows the taipan to take in more heat from the sun in cold weather.

El taipán del interior

El taipán del interior vive en desiertos donde hay muy poca vegetación. Se esconde entre las grietas y bajo las rocas. A menudo, las **escamas** de un taipán son más oscuras durante el invierno que en el verano. Esto les permite absorber el calor del sol cuando hace frio.

inland taipan/
taipán del interior

9

Laying Eggs

Female inland taipans lay 12 to 20 eggs at one time. They lay them in an animal den or a crack in the ground. Then they leave the eggs. The baby taipans break out of the eggs about 2 months later.

Poniendo huevos

Los taipanes hembra ponen de 12 a 20 huevos a la vez. Los ponen en la madriguera de algún animal o en una grieta en el suelo, y después los abandonan. Los taipanes bebé salen del huevo aproximadamente dos meses después.

Deadly!

All taipans are deadly snakes. They use **venom** to kill. The venom of the inland taipan is the strongest of any land snake on Earth. Just one bite has enough venom to kill 100 people! The venom can cause the taipan's **prey** to bleed to death.

- -

¡Serpiente mortal!

Todos los taipanes son mortales. Usan **veneno** para matar. El veneno del taipán del interior es el más fuerte de todas las serpientes terrestres del mundo. ¡Una sola mordida tiene suficiente veneno para matar a 100 personas! El veneno de un taipán puede desangrar a su **presa** hasta matarla.

13

Like most snakes, taipans have sharp teeth called fangs. They use their fangs to **inject** their venom into other animals. They do this to catch prey. They also do it to chase away enemies. Taipans sometimes bite people, but only when they're scared or trapped.

Como la mayoría de las serpientes, los taipanes tienen dientes afilados que se llaman colmillos. Los taipanes usan sus colmillos para **inyectar** el veneno en otros animales. Esto lo hacen para atrapar presas. También lo hacen para ahuyentar a sus enemigos. Los taipanes a veces muerden a la gente, pero solo cuando están asustados o se sienten acorralados.

15

Hungry?

Taipans eat birds, lizards, and **rodents**. Inland taipans mainly like to eat rats. Taipans hunt in the morning when it's cooler. During really hot weather, taipans hunt at night. A taipan **attacks** so quickly the prey often doesn't even see it!

¿Hambrientos?

Los taipanes comen pájaros, lagartijas y **roedores**. Los taipanes del interior prefieren comer ratas. Los taipanes cazan por la mañana cuando hace más fresco. Cuando hace mucho calor, los taipanes cazan durante la noche. ¡Un taipán **ataca** tan rápido que a menudo la presa no lo ve!

A taipan bite injects venom into its prey. Once a taipan bites its prey, it lets go and waits for the prey to die. The venom is strong and works fast. Once the prey is dead, the taipan eats it whole!

El taipán inyecta veneno en su presa cuando la muerde. Una vez que el taipán ha mordido a su presa, la suelta y espera a que muera. El veneno es muy fuerte y rápido. ¡En cuanto la presa está muerta, el taipán se la come entera!

19

Taipans and People

Taipans don't commonly attack people. However, they may attack if a person scares them or tries to catch them. Someone who is bitten by a taipan must take a drug called antivenin. This drug stops the venom from working. Without antivenin, the person will die.

Los taipanes y la gente

Normalmente, los taipanes no atacan a las personas. Sin embargo pueden atacar si la gente los asusta o trata de agarrarlos. Alguien que recibe una mordida de taipán tiene que tomarse un medicamento llamado antídoto. Este medicamento detiene los efectos del veneno. Sin antídoto, la persona morirá.

Snake Facts/
Hoja informativa

Inland Taipan/
El taipán del interior

Length/Longitud	about 5 feet (1.5 m) long unos 5 pies (1.5 m) de largo
Where It Lives/Hábitat	central desert of Australia desierto central de Australia
How Many Eggs a Female Lays/Cuantos huevos pone una hembra	12 to 20 at one time de 12 a 20 a la vez
Favorite Food/ Comida preferida	rats ratas
Killer Fact/ Datos mortales	A single bite from an inland taipan has enough venom to kill 100 adult people or 250,000 mice! ¡Una sola mordida de un taipán del interior tiene suficiente veneno para matar a 100 personas adultas o 250,000 ratones!

Glossary/Glosario

attack: to try to harm someone or something

inject: to use sharp teeth to force venom into an animal's body

prey: an animal hunted by other animals for food

rodent: a small, furry animal with large front teeth, such as a mouse or rat

scale: one of the plates that cover a snake's body

venom: something a snake makes in its body that can harm other animals

- -

atacar tratar de dañar a alguien o algo

escama (la) una de las láminas que cubre el cuerpo de una serpiente

inyectar usar dientes afilados para forzar veneno en el cuerpo de un animal

presa (la) un animal cazado por otro animal para comérselo

roedor (el) un animal pequeño y peludo con dientes frontales grandes, como un ratón o una rata

veneno (el) algo que produce una serpiente en su cuerpo que puede dañar a otros animales

For More Information/Más información

Books/Libros

Jenkins, Jennifer Meghan. *The 10 Deadliest Snakes.* Oakville, ON, Canada: Rubicon Publishers, 2007.

Wechsler, Doug. *Taipans.* New York, NY: PowerKids Press, 2001.

Web Sites/Páginas en Internet

Corwin's Quest: Inland Taipan

animal.discovery.com/videos/corwins-quest-inland-taipan.html
Snake expert Jeff Corwin tracks down an inland taipan.

Wild Recon: Coastal Taipan Venom

animal.discovery.com/videos/wild-recon-coastal-taipan-venom.html
Donald Schultz, host of Wild Recon, collects venom from a coastal taipan.

Index/Índice